To My Dearest
Ryan

With all of My Love,

Mom

12/2009

You're not just a fantastic son.
You're a tremendous, rare,
and extraordinary person.
And I couldn't be more proud of you...
if I tried.

— Douglas Pagels

# A Son

## Is Life's Greatest Gift

Words of Love and Advice
for a Son Any Parent
Would Be Proud Of

Edited by Gary Morris

**Blue Mountain Press**™
Boulder, Colorado

We wish to thank Susan Polis Schutz for permission to reprint the following poems that appear in this publication: "You Have Always Made Me So Proud," "Remember These Things, Son," "I Will Always Care About You and Your Happiness," "My Son, Always Stay the Unique Individual That You Are," and "To My Son, I Love You." Copyright © 1986, 1988, 1991, 1994 by Stephen Schutz and Susan Polis Schutz. And for "Whatever You Choose to Do with Your Life, I Will Be Proud of You." Copyright © 1979 by Continental Publications. All rights reserved.

Library of Congress Control Number: 2007907947
ISBN: 978-1-59842-313-6

Acknowledgments appear on page 92.

██ and Blue Mountain Press are registered in U.S. Patent and Trademark Office. Certain trademarks are used under license.

Printed in China.
First Printing: 2008

♻ This book is printed on recycled paper.

This book is printed on archival quality, white felt, 110 lb. paper. This paper has been specially produced to be acid free (neutral pH) and contains no groundwood or unbleached pulp. It conforms with all the requirements of the American National Standards Institute, Inc., so as to ensure that this book will last and be enjoyed by future generations.

# Blue Mountain Arts, Inc.

P.O. Box 4549, Boulder, Colorado 80306

# Contents

# Son,
# May These Words
# Always Remind You of
# My Love

*If ever you want to know*
*that someone in this world*
*thinks the sun rises when you smile*
*and that nothing is as amazing as your laugh.*
*If ever you feel the burden*
    *of guilt or failure*
        *and believe that no one*
*could love you just the way you are,*
    *then remember these words... because I do.*
*I love you exactly as you are.*

*When I gave birth to you,*
*the miracle never left my heart*
*and changed me forever.*
*Every second you are with me*
*is a gift no one could ever*
*put a price on.*
*So read these words...*
*and remember*
*you are the reason why*
*my life is so wonderful.*

— Renate M. Braddy

# To My Amazing, Remarkable Son

*Everywhere you journey in life, you will go with my love by your side.*

*Forever it will be with you. Truly, joyfully, and more meant to be than words could ever say. You are the joy of my life, the source of my dearest memories, the inspiration for my fondest wishes, and you are the sweetest present life could ever give to anyone.*

*I love you so much. I want you to remember that... every single day. And I want you to know that these are things I'll always hope and pray...*

*That the world will treat you fairly. That people will appreciate the one-in-a-million person you are. That you will be safe and smart and sure to make good choices on your journey through life.*

That a wealth of opportunities will come your way. That your blessings will be many, your troubles will be few, and that life will be very generous in giving you all the happiness and success you deserve.

You're not just a fantastic son. You're a tremendous, rare, and extraordinary person. All the different facets of your life — the ones you reveal to the rest of the world and the ones known only to those you're close to — are so impressive. And as people look even deeper, I know they can't help but see how wonderful you are inside.

I'll always love you, Son, with all my heart. And I couldn't be more proud of you... if I tried.

— Douglas Pagels

# I Think I've Been the Luckiest Parent of All

*I knew all along*
*that you had the makings*
   *of an angel;*
*from the moment you were born,*
*it has all been good news.*

*You make my life complete,*
*and I can't help but think*
*I'm the luckiest parent around.*
*Our closeness is a special gift;*
*our friendship is one of a kind.*
*Our bond is a circle of love*
*that never ends.*
*We made it through the tough years*
*by being willing to let miracles happen;*
*we've ridden the waves of life together.*
*It's not how much we've had*
    *but the love we've felt*
*that has made all the difference.*
*The stories in my heart... you wrote.*
*The memories I cherish... you created.*
*The happiness I feel... I owe to you.*
*In a very real way, you really are*
*here in my heart all the time.*

— *Linda E. Knight*

# Remember These Things, Son

*Always keep your many interests —*
*they will keep you*
*constantly occupied*
*Always keep your positive outlook —*
*it will give you the energy to*
*accomplish great things*
*Always keep your determination —*
*it will give you the ability*
*to succeed in meeting your goals*
*Always keep your excitement*
*about whatever you do —*
*it will help you to have fun*
*Always keep your sense of humor —*
*it will allow you to*
*make mistakes and learn from them*

*Always keep your confidence —*
*it will allow you to take risks*
*and not be afraid of failure*
*Always keep your sensitivity —*
*it will help you to understand*
*and do something about*
*injustices in the world*
*As you continue to grow*
*in your own unique, wonderful way*
*always remember that*
*I am more proud of you*
*than ever before and*
*I love you*

*— Susan Polis Schutz*

# A Little Thought
# I'd Love to Share
# with You

*I want your life to be such a wonderful one. I wish you peace, deep within your soul; joyfulness in the promise of each new day; stars to reach for, dreams to come true, and memories more beautiful than words can say.*

*I wish you friends close at heart, even over the miles; loved ones — the best treasures we're blessed with; present moments to live in, one day at a time; serenity, with its wisdom; courage, with its strength; and new beginnings, to give life a chance to really shine.*

*I wish you understanding — of how special you really are; a journey, safe from the storms and warmed by the sun; a path to wonderful things; an invitation to the abundance life brings; and an angel watching over, for all the days to come.*

*— Douglas Pagels*

# I Believe in You

*I know I'm your parent, but believe me when I say that you already possess all the qualities you'll ever need in this life. You're strong-willed and intelligent. You're kind and considerate. You make people feel good just by being around them.*

*I have complete faith in you, because I know that whatever choices you make in life will be the ones that are best for you.*

*So you see, you have no reason to ever be afraid of failing, because in my eyes... you're already a success!*

*— Jane Andrews*

# Son...

*Remember that rough-around-the-edges guy who used to stare back at you from the mirror? Take a fresh look, and maybe you'll see what the rest of us see. A young man with his feet on the ground and his eyes on the sky. A generous spirit and an open heart. And of course, that smile that just won't quit. Underneath it all, you have the courage to make your mark on the world in a way that is yours and yours alone.*

*Is it any wonder that the qualities that make you so very special are the same ones that make those who love you so very proud?*

*Never forget how amazing you are.*

— Rachel Snyder

# What It Means
# to Be a Man

*A man is someone who realizes
  that strength of character
is more important than being tough.*

*He can be tender and kind,
  and he doesn't misuse his authority.
He is generous, and enjoys
  giving as well as receiving.*

*A man is understanding;*
    *he tries to see both sides*
        *of a situation.*
*He is responsible;*
    *he knows what needs to be done,*
        *and he does it.*
*He is trustworthy; his word is his honor.*

*He loves humor and looks*
    *at the bright side of things.*
*He takes time to think before he reacts.*
*He loves life, nature, discovery,*
    *excitement, and so much more.*
*He is a little boy sometimes,*
    *living in an adult body*
*and enjoying the best of both worlds.*

— *Barbara Cage*

# My Son, Never Forget How Much I Love You

When you were very, very small
I used to dance with you
cradled in my arms.
You were my precious angel,
and when I held you close,
love overwhelmed me.

I used to wonder what kind of life
    you would lead.
What would be your first word,
    your first job?
What kind of man would you become?
And would your life take you
    far away from me?

Then I'd hold you even closer.
I'd give you an extra kiss
and an extra squeeze,
and whisper "I love you" one more time.

I knew you were too young to remember
   my words,
but I prayed you would never forget them.

Now you are a man.
There are days when I still long
   to cradle you in my arms
and dance with you once again.
Although I miss my little boy,
I am so proud of the man you are
and of who you will become.
When I think of you,
love still overwhelms me.
And as we both grow older
and memories fade,
please never forget these words
that you were once too small to remember:
"I love you."
             — *Kathryn Higginbottom Gorin*

# Be True to Yourself, Son

*B*e true to your dreams, and keep them alive. Never let anyone change your mind about what you feel you can achieve. Always believe in yourself.

*Be true to yourself in the paths that you choose. Follow your talents and passions; don't take the roads others say you must follow because they are the most popular. Take the paths where your talents will thrive — the ones that will keep your spirits alive with enthusiasm and everlasting joy.*

*Most of all, never forget that there is no brighter light than the one within you. Keep on being true to yourself. Keep shining your light on us so that we will always have a reason to smile. Follow your inner light to your own personal greatness, and remember that we admire you and love you just as you are.*

*— Jacqueline Schiff*

# In My Eyes, Son, You Shine as Bright as a New Star

*In your eyes,*
*I know sometimes you find fault*
*in the things you do,*
*and you are uncertain about*
*some of your choices.*
*You may wonder if you can make it*
*through the tough times*
*and if you can make your*
*beautiful dreams come true.*

*I want you to know that in my eyes,*
*you have the ability,*
*determination, and strength*
*to make them all come true.*
*I see who you really are:*
*a doer, an achiever, a winner.*

*I see all the spirit, the potential,*
*the hopes, and the dreams*
*that grow in your heart.*
*I watch you work hard and*
*give it your all in everything you do.*
*I know you will strive and thrive.*
*I believe you will find as much happiness*
*as your heart can hold,*
*and you will travel as far*
*as your dreams can take you.*
*In my eyes,*
*you shine as bright as a new star —*
*and with my whole heart*
*I believe in you*
*and all that you can be.*

— *Vickie M. Worsham*

# You Have Always
# Made Me So Proud

*I am so happy
with the direction
that your life
is taking you*

*All of your decisions and*
*all of your actions*
*are so noble and intelligent*
*I often think about*
*how you were the same way*
*when you were a little boy*
*I hope that you remain*
*    so in control*
*of your life forever*
*I want you to know that*
*sometimes you will make mistakes*
*and when those times occur*
*the proudest parent in the world*
*is always here*
*to encourage you*
*to understand you*
*to talk with you*
*to support you*
*    and to love you forever*

*— Susan Polis Schutz*

# Like Every
# Other Parent...

*I wonder if I've done all the right things for you and if what I haven't done will do you harm. I wonder if I've told you enough times how special you are and that it's okay to be "you," no matter what others might say.*

*I wonder if I've made certain that you know there isn't anything you could say or do which would ever turn me away from you. I pray that our home was and still is a safe haven for you, where you can find refuge after a long day of discovering yourself.*

*I wonder if I've let you know enough about me. Have I shared stories about my own childhood and adolescence, about my vulnerabilities, my mistakes, my fears — and then reassured you that it all turned out okay? Have I let you see me feel foolish and humbled? Have I taught you to laugh at yourself even when others are laughing too? Have I shown you that nothing is so impossible it can't be tried?*

*As I am with you less and less, I hope you remember all that we've built together and it helps you face new challenges we haven't experienced. I know now all I can do is begin to let you go and trust that we have been good for each other — the times we've spent together were gifts to me.*

*I hope someday, when you look back on your life, it will seem rich for the love, care, and time we've shared together. I hope you become a seeker of truth and beauty and learn to listen with your heart. You will always be in mine.*

— Lisa Crofton

# I Just Want to Remind You, Son...

*Though time has lessened
your reliance on me,
prompting you to be more dependent
on your own good instincts in life,
I feel you should know
that I'm always here for you.*

*I know that you have everything*
*in your life under control.*
*You're doing fine, and nothing is*
*bothering you or standing in*
*your way right now.*
*There's no way to describe this feeling*
*of pride in my heart for the way*
*your life is going.*

*But I felt like reminding you once more,*
*the way parents like to do,*
*that I'm still here to listen when you*
*feel like talking things over or if you*
*need someone to lean on for a while.*
*You'll always be my son,*
*and I'll love and care about you*
*your whole life through.*

*— Barbara J. Hall*

# I Hope You Will
# Always Choose Wisely

Decisions are incredibly important things!
Good decisions will come back to bless you.
Bad decisions can come back to haunt you.

That's why it's so important that you take the
time to choose wisely.

Choose to do the things that will reflect well...
on your ability, your integrity, your spirit, your
health, your tomorrows,
    your smiles,
    your dreams, and yourself.

You are such a wonder. You're the only one
in the universe exactly like you! I want you to
take care of that rare and remarkable soul.

*I want you to know that there is someone who will thank you for doing the things you do now with foresight and wisdom and respect.*

*It's the person you will someday be.*

*You have a chance to make that person so thankful and so proud. All you have to do is remember one of the lessons I learned when I made a similar journey. It's pretty simple, really, just these nine little words:*

> *Each time you come to a crossroads*
> *...choose wisely.*

*— Douglas Pagels*

*All* who have accomplished
great things
have had a great aim
and fixed their gaze
on a goal which was high —
one which sometimes seemed
impossible.

— *Orison Swett Marden*

# Son, You Must Find Your Own Path in Life

*I* *will not say to you:*
  *"This is the Way; walk in it."*
*For I do not know your way*
  *or where the Spirit may call you.*
*Just this I say:*
*I know for every truth there is a way*
  *for each of us to walk,*
    *a right for each of us to choose,*
      *and a truth to use.*
*And though you wander far, your soul*
*will know the true path when you find it.*

*— Author Unknown*

# Son, May Your World Be Filled with Love

*The world is full of love; there is no end to it. And if you have it in your life, you'll find yourself capable of achieving great things.*

*Remember there are many different kinds of love; don't neglect any of them, for each will add something different and unique to your days. Open yourself to every experience, and don't be afraid to reveal your feelings. If it's in your nature to be a romantic, allow yourself to fully and freely express it; you may discover talents and gifts within you that you never could have found in any other way.*

*Don't ever let the actions of other people
lead you to shut off your own emotions or
hesitate to put your faith in love. Give your
relationships the very best that's in you —
remembering as you do that all the love you
give away just increases your own capacity
for receiving even more in return someday.*

*Always look at the world with loving eyes,
and you'll find love reflected back to you from
every corner of your days. Your heart can
be a catalyst for changing the world as long
as you treat everyone you meet in kind and
loving ways.*

*Remember it is your destiny to be a strong,
loving, happy man — and you will be, if you
always walk the path of life with an open
and trusting heart, and give yourself to love.*

*— Avery Jakobs*

# When You Dream,
# My Son...
# Dream Deep

**W**hen you love, make it last.
When you have hopes, hold on
to them with all your heart. Your
possibilities are unsurpassed.

When you share, share completely. When thoughts wander, let them soar. When your wishes come up empty, don't give up on them. Your opportunities might be just behind the next door.

When you deal with difficulties, keep your courage. When you awaken, remember that each sunrise is brand-new. When you travel toward tomorrow, choose your own direction. Your happiness will always help to guide you.

When special feelings come your way, let them flow into your heart. When miracles try to find you, don't hide. When special people come along, let them know what a blessing they are. Smiles begin way down deep inside.

— Collin McCarty

# I Will Always
# Care About You
# and Your Happiness

*My son*
*I want you to have a life of happiness*
*In order for you to have this*
*you must have many interests*
*and pursue them*
*You must have many goals*
*and work toward them*
*You must like your work*
*and always try to get better*
*You must consider yourself a success*
*by being proud of doing your best*
*You must have fun every day*
*You must listen to your own voice*
*and not be influenced by others*

*You must have someone who is*
*worthy of you to love*
*and to share your life*
*You must have peace*
*and not always expect perfection*
*You must have respect*
*for yourself and others*
*My son, as I watch you grow up*
*I can see you are on the right path*
*and I am so proud of you*
*I will always care about you*
*and your happiness*
*I love you*

— Susan Polis Schutz

# My Love for You
# Won't Ever Change

*I remember when you were small*
*and bumped your head*
*or scraped your knee.*
*I was the one you came running to —*
*so sure I would take away the hurt*
*and "make it better" with a kiss.*

Whether it was missing homework,
    a broken toy,
or a loose button on your shirt,
it gave me such a good feeling
to be able to "fix" what was wrong
with your world.

Now you're grown up.
You still have hurts
and things still go wrong
    in your world,
and I wish so much that I
could "make things better"
the way I could when you
were a little boy.
Most of your hurts are the kind
that can't be cured with a kiss
and a bandage,
but one thing hasn't changed...

my love for you.

— Dawn E. McCormick

# I Never Thought You'd Grow Up So Fast

When you started kissing me on the cheek instead of jumping into my arms, I began to wonder. When you no longer squealed with delight when I walked in the door, I started to guess. When you put away your dinosaurs and began picking out your own clothes, I was pretty sure. When you hid behind your menu because the waitress was a girl you knew from school — that's when I knew my little boy had somehow grown up to be a man right before my eyes.

I had thought that if I watched you closely enough or held you tightly enough, you'd be my little boy forever.

*But time has wings of its own and soars beyond a parent's feelings — carrying a son from toothless grins and the smell of baby powder to driver's education and filling out college applications.*

*I always knew this day would come. Somehow I thought I'd be ready... but what parent is ever prepared to see her baby take flight? As you navigate your way through the endless maze that will become your life, always remember — there is no distance that can ever separate us or any space between your heart and mine.*

*— Kimberly O'Bryan*

# When You Were Little, Son...

*All* I ever wanted was to see your happy face. It isn't really much different today.

In your smiles,
I still want to see
the understanding that you are loved.
I want to see the boy beneath
the man you have become,
able to be himself at any age.
I want your days to be bright
from beginning to end...
as bright as my life has been
since you entered it.
What I wish most of all for you
is a life filled with whatever
    makes you happy,
because your happiness
    and being with you
are all I've ever wanted.

— Carole Conner Davis

# A Son...

*tickles your funny bone* ⟵ *musters courage to fight off huge creatures, imaginary and non-imaginary* ⟵ *tracks mud into the house after you've cleaned the carpet* ⟵ *"drives" his tricycle like a big rig* ⟵ *fishes without worms* ⟵ *climbs the tallest tree in the yard, and then falls out of it* ⟵ *names the frog in the garden after his grandma* ⟵ *becomes the "cookie monster"* ⟵ *paints the newly painted wall with crayons* ⟵ *scratches your back* ⟵ *steals the neighbor's flowers for your Mother's Day gift* ⟵ *puts the blue in blue skies and takes away all the gray ones* ⟵ *becomes a jack-of-all-trades when he's eight years old* ⟵ *secretly loves his parents* ⟵ *is self-sufficient at an early age* ⟵

A son likes landscaping, but not maintenance ⇐
dances in private ⇐ calls you three more
times at work after you've told him not to call
anymore ⇐ can put anything together without
instructions ⇐ takes everything apart that can
be separated ⇐ trades your stereo for the broken
one without telling you ⇐ eats two sandwiches
an hour before dinner ⇐ cracks a rib, but never
lets you see him cry ⇐ vacuums the cat ⇐
accepts collect calls from anybody ⇐ pretends
to be aloof until he kisses his mother's cheek ⇐
melts your heart every day of his life ⇐

— Linda Robertson

# Although You Are
# a Man Now...

*I hope you will never forget*
*the child within you.*
*That child will never grow up*
*and will help you keep humor,*
*spontaneity, and trust in your life.*

*Others may try to place*
*expectations on you —*
*even loved ones and friends —*
*and you may feel under pressure*
*to fulfill them.*
*Harder still, you may perhaps*
*place expectations on yourself*
*and feel that you've failed*
*when you don't meet them.*
*But I have learned that*
*expectations cannot always be reached;*
*the best that you can ever do*
*is fulfill the vision you hold in your heart.*
*Finally, I want to say that*
*I will always be here for you —*
*to honor your growth as a person*
*and your journey in life*
*wherever it takes you —*
*because I love you.*

*— Stephanie June Sorrell*

# My Son, Always Stay the Unique Individual That You Are

Men are told by society that
they must always be strong
They are told to block out
all sensitive, "unmanly" feelings
Men are told that
they must be leaders
they must achieve
they must succeed in a career
They are judged their whole lives
by the power they have
and how much money they earn

*My son, I hope you will never*
*feel pressured by society*
*You should be free to think*
*and do whatever you want*
*and to act the way you feel at all times*
*You should cry when you want to*
*and laugh when you want to*
*You should just be*
*the outstanding person*
*that you are —*
*the person that I am so proud of*
*and whom I love always*

*— Susan Polis Schutz*

# Life Is Everything
# You Make It...
# and More

*As you grow and experience more things in your life, know that there will inevitably be obstacles to encounter. But don't worry that they will seem too great for you to handle, because you can.*

*You may doubt yourself at times, but know that if you have faith, you have everything. Faith is the key to being successful.*

*If you know you are capable of anything because of who you are, you will always reach your destination. It may not always be easy, but it will always be worth it. Look ahead of you, never behind. Have faith in yourself. If you do, you will be amazed at what you can accomplish.*

*Remember, Son, life is what you make it... and more.*

*— T. L. Nash*

# You Can
# Accomplish Anything

In my thoughts,
I see you standing as you really are —
powerful, sensitive, determined,
    and gracious.
I can see you achieving everything
    you choose to achieve.
I can see you being exactly
who and what you want to be.
Look through my eyes for an instant,
and you'll see yourself
conquering all limitations.
Look through my eyes
and see who you really are
and what you are capable of.
You can accomplish anything —
    I know you can.

— Lea Marie Tomlyn

# There Is Greatness Within You

*Throughout your life, I hope you will always
pursue sensitivity and kindness
    as your chosen way.
Your sense of humor is wonderful;
    hold on to it.
Being able to laugh at the world
    will see you through many hard times.
Guard against bitterness and sarcasm;
    they can destroy you.
Be yourself; the world will benefit
    from your talent and your humor.
Search for people who love and
    appreciate you for who you are
and who encourage you to improve.
Don't be satisfied with less
    than all you can be,
for you have greatness within you.*

— Bill Cross

# Whatever You Choose to Do with Your Life, I Will Be Proud of You

*It is so important
to choose your own
lifestyle
and not let others
choose it for you*

Do what you want to do
Be what you want to be
Look the way you want to look
Act the way you want to act
Think the way you want to think
Speak the way you want to speak
Follow the goals you want to follow

Live according to the truths
  within yourself
and know that whatever you do
I am here to support you
and always feel very proud of you

— Susan Polis Schutz

# You've Made All
# My Days So Happy

The day you were born
was one of the happiest days of my life.

I remember counting
your tiny fingers and toes
and cradling you in my arms,
certain that I would never let you go.
But let you go, I did —
into the big wide world,
into the life that you
would make for yourself.
I have been so proud
as I've watched you grow:
proud of the care you show to others,
of the love you have for your family,
and of the integrity with which
you live your life.

*I wish I could have held on to you*
*for a little longer.*
*I wish that children didn't have to grow up*
*and leave home.*
*But I know that you are just as important*
*to other people as you are to me,*
*and I feel lucky*
*to have had you for as long as I did.*

*Now my gifts to you no longer come*
*in boxes filled with building blocks*
*or toy trains,*
*but rather in the memories that we share*
*and in the love that keeps growing*
*as the years go by.*

*May every day bring you*
*a reason to celebrate.*
*May you be surrounded*
*by those you love.*
*May each day of your life*
*be filled with happiness.*

— *Lea Walsh*

# Your Family Is Always Here for You

*Family is a feeling of*
*belonging and acceptance.*
*It's a safe retreat, a shelter,*
*and an instant connection*
*to the people who have*
*    faith in you —*
*that wonderful circle*
*of lifelong friends*
*and the smiles that go*
*straight to your heart with love.*

Anything that touches your life
    touches theirs, too.
They care, and they show it.
You don't even need to explain;
they understand,
and they are there for you.

A family is a special source
    of well-being —
full of people who hold you
    in the roughest times,
share your life,
and love to be there for you.
And even if you don't
    say it often enough...
you appreciate and love them
    so much.
                — Barbara J. Hall

# My Son, There Is No Limit to Your Future

You have the ability
to attain whatever you seek;
within you is every potential
you can imagine.
Always aim higher than
you believe you can reach.
So often, you'll discover
that when your talents
are set free
by your imagination,
you can achieve any goal.
If people offer
their help or wisdom
as you go through life,
accept it gratefully.

*You can learn much from those*
*who have gone before you.*
*But never be afraid or hesitant*
*to step off the accepted path*
*and head off in your own direction*
*if your heart tells you*
*it's the right way for you.*
*Always believe that you will*
*ultimately succeed*
*at whatever you do,*
*and never forget the value*
*of persistence, discipline,*
*and determination.*
*You are meant to be*
*whatever you dream*
*of becoming.*

*— Edmund O'Neill*

*Twenty years from now you will be more disappointed by the things you didn't do than by the ones you did do. So throw off the bowlines. Sail away from the safe harbor. Catch the trade winds in your sails. Explore. Dream. Discover.*

— Mark Twain

# I Know You
# Will Be a Success

What does it mean to succeed? Most people see success as being rich and famous or powerful and influential. Others see it as being at the top of their profession and standing out from the rest.

The wise see success in a more personal way; they see it as achieving the goals they have set for themselves, and then feeling pride and satisfaction in their accomplishments. True success is felt in the heart, not measured by money and power.

So be true to yourself and achieve the goals you set. For success is reaching those goals and feeling proud of what you have accomplished.

— Tim Tweedie

# You Were Born to Shine

You are just as special as anyone else, just as talented and gifted, so don't hide your light, your heart, your gifts. Let them shine.

Don't be afraid; your talents won't let you down. Don't worry; you can't fail at what you were born for. You have what it takes! Find your passion, polish it daily, and use it to make your dreams come true. (You can do it!)

You may not see yourself as a star or feel like one. But our feelings have a habit of misleading us sometimes; they often prevent us from seeing ourselves in a true light. You actually possess more star qualities than you can imagine; you're capable of achieving much more than you think. So don't listen to your fears or doubts. Ignore them and they will get out of your way.

*Focus on what you can accomplish and give it
everything you have. Good things will happen.
Doors will open. You can count on it!*

*In the heavens there are billions of stars. Each
has its own unique beauty, light, and purpose.
So do you! On the stage of life where we live,
everyone who lets their light shine is a star
and a winner, too. Don't diminish your own
light by comparing it to others. Remember that
other stars only help us to shine brighter and
be more beautiful.*

*As it is impossible to count the stars, so too
is it impossible for you to know the depth of
wonderful things that could happen if you step
out in faith and dare to let your light shine.
Take that chance! Someone is going to see
your light and be blessed — and so will you.
And that is what you were born for. You were
born to shine.*

*— Nancye Sims*

# Son, I Want to Give You the Gifts That Last Forever

*I want to give you
the kinds of gifts that will last
your whole life through,
things that you just
can't put a price tag on.*

*I want to give you*
*the courage to*
*stand up for what you believe in;*
*a level head; a warm heart;*
*a sense of humor*
*to get you through any situation;*
*the ability to keep*
*growing and learning*
*as life brings changes;*
*a positive outlook for the future;*
*the love and support*
*of friends and family;*
*and the confidence and inspiration*
*to follow your dreams*
*wherever they may take you.*

— *Morgan R. Gray*

# I Would Do
# Anything for You

*If I could bring you a world full of happiness, I would. If I could take your sadness and pain and feel them for you, I would. If I could give you the strength to handle the problems that this world may have for you, I'd do that, too. There is nothing that I wouldn't do for you to bring laughter instead of tears into your life.*

*I can't give you happiness, but I can feel it with you. I can't take away all your hurts in this world, but I can share them with you. I can't give you strength when you need it the most, but I can try to be strong for you.*

*I can be there to tell you how much I love you. In times when you feel you need to reach out to someone, I can be there for you — not to change how you feel, but to go through these times with you.*

*When you were little, I could hold you in my arms to comfort you, but you'll never be too grown up for me to put my arms around you. You are so very special to me, and the most precious gift I could have ever received was you on the day you were born. I love you!*

*— Millie P. Lorenz*

# For You,
# My Wonderful Son

What's most important in
my life, and the things that
make me happiest,
are all found in one
perfect place:
in my family.

Whenever I see you, I know I am looking at the smiling face of one of the most remarkable people I will ever have the privilege of knowing.

I find these "it-doesn't-get-any-better-than-this" feelings inside me all the time, and they bring so much sweetness into my world.

I am more thankful for you than I can ever say, and I want you to know...

If I could be given any gift imaginable, one that would make me happy beyond words, make me feel truly blessed, and make my days just shine...

The gift I'd choose... would be you.

Each and every time.

— Terry Bairnson

You have so many moments ahead of you, Son... days that will bring new people into your life and times that will bring new friends into your world.

Having had the wonderful pleasure of knowing you (since the minute you were born!) and appreciating the million and one things that are so wonderful about you...

I will always hope that the people
who share your life are
special, insightful people who
realize how lucky they are
to be in the presence
of a present
like you.

— Marta Best

# When Problems
# Overwhelm You...

Carry on as I would, Son.
Lay your problems down to rest.
Put all bad times behind you
and strive to be your best.

Carry on with confidence;
your hands now hold the reins.
Don't think your talents won't compare,
for my blood runs through your veins.

Carry on with honesty;
you know what's right and fair.
Just call on me when problems strike;
you know that I'll be there.

Carry on the dream, Son.
Let your conscience be your guide.
Remember when you feel alone,
I'm standing by your side.

— Shelley McDaniel

# To My Son,
# I Love You

*I feel so fortunate to have you for a son*
*I love your bright face*
*when we talk seriously about the world*
*I love your smile*
*when you laugh at the inconsistencies*
*  in the world*

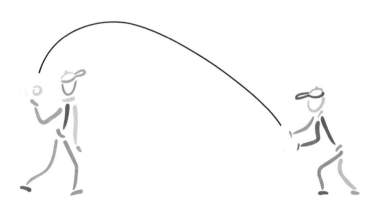

*I love your eyes*
*when you are showing emotion*
*I love your mind*
*when you are discovering new ideas*
*and creating dreams to follow*
*Many people tell me that*
*they cannot talk to their children*
*that they cannot wait for them*
*   to leave home*
*I want you to know*
*that I enjoy you so much and*
*I look forward to any time we can*
*   spend together*
*I am so proud of you*
*my son and*
*I love you*
                    *— Susan Polis Schutz*

# No Matter
# How Old You Are...

Your happiness, health, and safety
mean everything to me.

I always think of you as my child
and love you as much as ever.

I enjoy being with you
and am very pleased at the person
you've turned out to be.

Your voice is one of my favorite sounds,
and your laughter always delights me.

You should always believe
that you are capable and worthy,
precious and unique —
    and act accordingly.

*You have touched my heart*
*and made me proud*
*more often than you could imagine.*

*Memories of you are very dear to me,*
*and sharing special times and traditions*
*makes them all the more enjoyable.*

*You bless my life in so many ways,*
*and I am thankful for the friendship*
*that we share.*

*There is nothing you could ever do*
*to lessen my love for you.*

*Being your parent has given me*
*happiness to the greatest degree*
*and warmth that fills my heart.*
*I am in awe that you came into my life*
*and made my dreams come true.*

*— Barbara Cage*

# The Bond Between Parents and Sons Lasts a Lifetime

*It remains unchanged by time or distance.*
*It is the purest love —*
*unconditional and true.*
*It is understanding of any situation*
*and forgiving of any mistake.*

*It is strong enough to withstand*
*harsh words and hurt feelings,*
*for it is smart enough to always*
*see the love beyond the words.*
*It is brave enough to always*
*    speak the truth,*
*even when lies would be easier.*
*It is always there —*
*    anytime, anywhere —*
*whenever it is needed.*
*It is a gift held in the heart*
*    and in the soul,*
*and it cannot be taken away*
*or exchanged for another.*
*To possess this love is a treasure*
*that makes life more valuable.*

*— Stephanie Douglass*

# I Hope You'll Keep on Making Your Greatest Dreams Come True

You are bright, talented, and creative. You have a spirit of adventure and an intense desire to make the world better. You are sensitive to the needs of others and passionate about helping people. You are driven to reach dreams that will make your future so much brighter. You have an inner spark that kindles a light in everyone your life touches.

You are a precious gift to the present and the future, and you must never forget this. Keep on flying with your highest dreams, and believe they will carry you where you want to go. Say "yes" to challenges, and dare to make those big, bold dreams come true.

*Tend the fires of your passions and use
this energy to do good in life. Stand up
for what is right. Protest the negative
things in this world that damage the gifts
of the heart. When you see a wrong, be
strong in speaking out. Be committed in
your friendships with those who need
a friend the most. Be a volunteer and
a positive leader.*

*Keep your good character, high ideals,
and deepest passions alive and active.
Fly on the wings of your talents and your
mightiest dreams. Strive to change the
world one day at a time. And as you fly,
carry a picture of me smiling at you with
my brightest love and my deepest pride.*

— *Jacqueline Schiff*

# I Want You to Know How Much You Mean to Me

Sometimes I can hardly believe
that the man I see when I look at you
used to be my little boy.
Where did the time go?
How did the moments turn into years
that disappeared behind us
at such great speed?

I am in awe at the changes that
have taken place in you,
and sometimes it saddens me
because that part of my life is over.
Yet I also feel the happiness
and pride in having a son
who is all grown up,
and nothing can dull or dampen
the wonderful memories I have
of you as my little boy.
The pride I have in you
and the love I feel for you
have continued to grow,
much like you have.
If you could look inside my heart
and see the love there,
if you could feel its strength and depth,
then you would know that you
have fulfilled my life in ways
no other person ever could.

— Barbara Cage

# Son, I'm Very Proud of You

There have been moments when all I wanted to do was hold you in my arms and tell you everything would be all right. But as a parent, sometimes my job was more than just giving a reassuring hug.

I had to let you find out things for yourself, even when the outcome was painful. It wasn't always easy, but I believed it was necessary.

If I allowed you to think that any problem you ever had would go away just by wishful thinking, I wouldn't have been fulfilling my role as a parent. You had to learn and grow through your own trials and experiences — slowly but surely building self-confidence and courage with every step you took.

*I encouraged you to be yourself, feel comfortable with who you are, and not let any obstacle in front of you frighten you away. I tried to teach you courage and positive thinking to guide you over uncertain waters.*

*I did the best I could with whatever tools I had. I wasn't a perfect parent, but I tried. And through all the tears and the worrying, you turned out just fine. You're successful, intelligent, and there is no limit to where you can go or what you can do. But more than just your accomplishments got you to where you are today. Good morals, a sense of humor, and a loving heart contribute to the wonderful man you are.*

*I love you, and I want you to know how proud I am of you.*

*— T. L. Nash*

# A Son Is
# Life's Greatest Gift

*Some people can only wish on stars —*
*but I have your star*
*shining here in my heart,*
*and the magic of your presence*
*in my life*
*makes every season*
*even more wonderful.*

Our days together haven't all
   been easy ones;
the years haven't always been smooth.
But there isn't a gift in all the world
that could ever outshine you.
The day you were born, I saw my future
all wrapped up in every memory.
You fill my heart with treasures
every single day.
I look at you and my eyes fill with tears.
Spending time with you is where
my best memories begin.
I stop to count my blessings
whenever I think of you.
A son's love is one-of-a-kind...
and you are the best son
any heart could ever hope for.

— Linda E. Knight

# ACKNOWLEDGMENTS

We gratefully acknowledge the permission granted by the following authors and authors' representatives to reprint poems or excerpts from their publications.

Rachel Snyder for "Son...." Copyright © 2007 by Rachel Snyder. All rights reserved.

Vickie M. Worsham for "In My Eyes, Son, You Shine as Bright as a New Star." Copyright © 2008 by Vickie M. Worsham. All rights reserved.

Lisa Crofton for "Like Every Other Parent...." Copyright © 2008 by Lisa Crofton. All rights reserved.

Kimberly O'Bryan for "I Never Thought You'd Grow Up So Fast." Copyright © 2008 by Kimberly O'Bryan. All rights reserved.

Linda Robertson for "A Son...." Copyright © 2008 by Linda Robertson. All rights reserved.

Barbara J. Hall for "Your Family Is Always Here for You." Copyright © 2008 by Barbara J. Hall. All rights reserved.

Nancye Sims for "You Were Born to Shine." Copyright © 2008 by Nancye Sims. All rights reserved.

Linda E. Knight for "A Son Is Life's Greatest Gift." Copyright © 2008 by Linda E. Knight. All rights reserved.

A careful effort has been made to trace the ownership of selections used in this anthology in order to obtain permission to reprint copyrighted material and give proper credit to the copyright owners. If any error or omission has occurred, it is completely inadvertent, and we would like to make corrections in future editions provided that written notification is made to the publisher:

BLUE MOUNTAIN ARTS, INC., P.O. Box 4549, Boulder, Colorado 80306.